FOSS Next Generation

Science Resources

Full Option Science System
Developed at
The Lawrence Hall of Science,
University of California, Berkeley
Published and distributed by
Delta Education,
a member of the School Specialty Family

1511919
978-1-62571-446-6
Printing 7 — 6/2017
Webcrafters, Madison, WI

FOSS Science Resources

Physical Science

FOSS Science Resources

Solids and Liquids

Table of Contents

Everything Matters

The world is made up of many things. Trees, bubbles, slides, and drinking fountains are just some of them. These things may all seem very different. But in one way, they are all the same. They are all **matter**. Matter is anything that takes up space.

Matter can be divided into three groups called
states. They are **solid**, **liquid**, and **gas**.

A slide is a solid.

Water is a liquid.

Bubbles are filled with **air**. Air is a gas.
How did the gas get into the bubbles?

Gases are hard to see and feel. You can't
hold gas in your hand or see it in a bucket.
How can you see gas?

Air is gas, and air is all around. You can see
air make a windmill spin. Which windmills
show air at work?

A helium balloon is fun. Helium is a kind of gas. It is lighter than air. What happens when you let go of a helium balloon? It floats away.

We use solids and liquids all the time.
Every solid and liquid is different. So
they are useful in different ways.

Cement bricks are strong and hard.
They are just right for building walls.

Wool is soft and flexible. It is good for hats and scarves.

Water can spray and splash. It makes
a hot summer day lots of fun!

Look around you for solids and liquids.
How will you use them today?

Solid Objects and Materials

Chairs are solid **objects**.
Blocks are solid objects.
So are chopsticks.

Chairs, blocks, and chopsticks are all different. We sit on chairs. We build with blocks. We eat with chopsticks.

Chairs, blocks, and chopsticks are all the same, too. They are all made of the same **material**. They are all made of wood.

Wood has good **properties** for making chairs. Wood is strong and rigid.

But wood is not a good material for making socks. What material has good properties for socks?

Fabric is a good material for socks. Fabric is soft and flexible. Fabric is a good material for shirts and blankets, too.

Kick balls are solid objects. Rubber is a good material for kick balls. Rubber stretches, and it is strong.

Rubber is a good material for making tires and balloons, too.

Some shoes are made of fabric, rubber, and metal. Some shoes are made of the material leather. Leather is strong and flexible.

Shoes are solid objects. This shoe is made of three different materials. Can you see all three materials?

Jars are solid objects. This jar is made of two materials. Can you see the two materials?

The jar is made of the material plastic. Plastic is strong and light. The label is made of the material paper. Paper is light and flexible.

Windows are solid objects. Windows are made of the material glass. Glass is strong and **transparent**.

What other objects are made of glass?

Cars are solid objects. Cars are made of many materials. How many different materials can you see?

Thinking about Solid Objects and Materials

1. What material would be good for making an umbrella?

2. How many materials are used to make a pencil?

3. How are materials different from objects?

Towers

This is a **tower**. It is called a communication tower. It is rigid and tall. The base is wider than the top. It can stand by itself. It has a very strong steel frame.

This fire lookout tower is on a mountaintop in the forest. It is a tall structure. Forest rangers use it to look for forest fires. The lookout tower is rigid and has a wide base. A forest ranger can see the whole forest from the top.

One of the most famous towers in the world is the Eiffel Tower. It was built in Paris, France, over 120 years ago. The tower's wide base and narrow body make the Eiffel Tower very stable.

This structure is in Seattle, Washington. It is called the Space Needle. It is tall and rigid. It has a wide, strong, and heavy base. Do you think it is a tower?

Bridges

A **bridge** connects two landmasses. Bridges usually go over water.

The picture shows the Golden Gate Bridge. This bridge carries a road across San Francisco Bay in California.

Two long steel cables hold up the roadway. Two huge towers support the steel cables.

The Tower Bridge connects the two sides of a river in England. It is two bridges in one. The lower bridge is a roadway that rises to let large boats pass. People walk on the upper bridge to cross the river.

Here is a simple bridge in a meadow. What
materials is the bridge made from? How is
the bridge supported?

A bridge allows you to walk over a creek without getting your feet wet. What are the parts of this bridge?

This bridge helps people walk across the canyon safely. Steel cables hold up the narrow footpath.

Liquids

They can splash. They can squirt. They can bubble and fizz. They come in many colors. What are they? Liquids!

Liquids can spill. Liquids can flow. That's why liquids have to be kept in containers. Glasses, bottles, and tank trucks are containers.

Do you know what the largest
liquid container in the world is?
It's the ocean!

Liquids flow. That's why they can change shape.
These four glasses are the same size and shape.
Each glass has the same amount of liquid.

These containers are different sizes and shapes.
Let's pour liquid from three of the glasses into
the containers.

The water looks different! It is a different shape.
The same amount of water can be tall and thin.
It can be short and wide.

Liquids change shape in each kind of container.

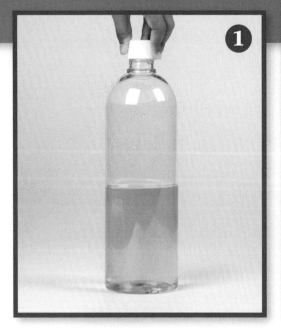

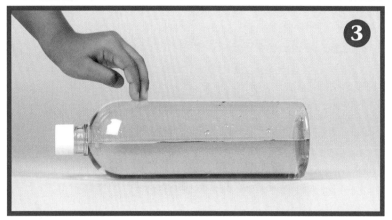

Liquids always move to the bottom of a container.
The liquid is in the bottom of this bottle.

Look at the pictures of the bottle turning over.
Compare pictures 1 and 3. Did the liquid move?
Or did the bottle move? What is different about
the liquid in all the pictures?

What is the same about the liquid in all the pictures? Look at the line near the **surface** of the liquid. It doesn't matter how you turn the bottle. The surface is always flat and level.

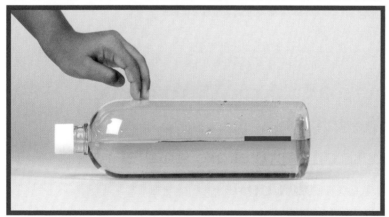

Pouring

Rocks are solid objects. This mountain
is a giant rock. Boulders are big rocks.
River rocks and gravel are smaller rocks
that you can pick up.

A piece of sand is a tiny rock. We call pieces of sand **particles**. You can put millions of sand particles in a bucket.

Sand can pour out of a bucket. Is sand a liquid or a solid?

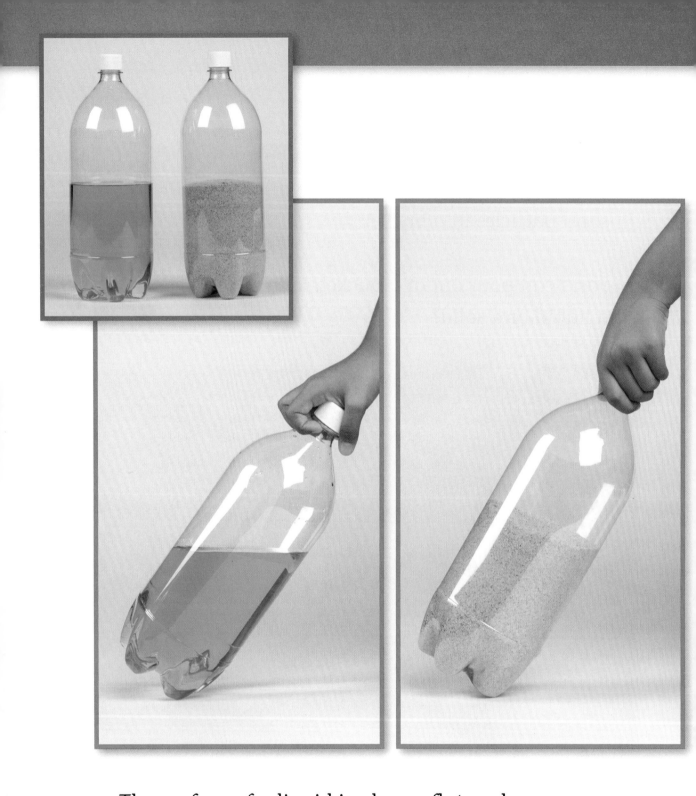

The surface of a liquid is always flat and level. Is the surface of sand flat? Is the surface of sand level?

Heavy, solid objects **sink** in liquids.
Do heavy objects sink in sand?

What happens when you pour sand and water on a hard surface? The sand makes a pile. But the water flows and spreads out.

Here are some other materials that pour.
Are they solids or liquids?

Comparing Solids and Liquids

What is the difference between solids and liquids? They have different properties. Properties describe how something looks or feels.

Shape and size are two properties of solid objects. The shape and size don't change unless you do something to the objects. Solids can be rigid, like a bat. When something is rigid, you can't bend it.

Solids can be flexible, like a sweater. When something is flexible, you can bend and stretch it.

Some solids can be broken into pieces. Each piece has a different shape and takes up less space.

What happens when you put the pieces back together? The solid has the same shape as before. It takes up the same space, too.

Solid objects can be very small, like sand.
You can pour sand out of a bucket. But
every grain of sand is a solid.

Liquids have properties, too. A liquid can be poured. It doesn't have its own shape. It takes the shape of the container that holds it.

A liquid has a different shape in each different container.

Liquids can be **foamy**, **bubbly**, or transparent.
They can be **translucent** or **viscous**.

viscous

translucent

foamy

bubbly and transparent

53

Solids and liquids are all around you. Can you find the solids in each picture? Can you find the liquids?

Mix It Up!

When you put together two or more things, you get a **mixture**.

Can you see what things make up this mixture?

What happens when you mix two liquids?

It depends. Sometimes the liquids mix together to make one new liquid.

Sometimes they don't mix. The two liquids form layers.

What happens when you mix a solid with a liquid?

It depends. Solids like marbles just get wet. A solid like a cookie falls apart. It breaks into smaller pieces.

A solid like salt disappears in a liquid.
It **dissolves**. The salt breaks apart into
tiny pieces. The pieces are so small you
can't see them.

How can you find out if the salt is there? If you
wait long enough, the liquid will **evaporate**.
The water will go into the air. The salt is left
behind in the form of **crystals**.

Solids and liquids are everywhere. We use them every day. How are solids being used here?

How are liquids being used here?

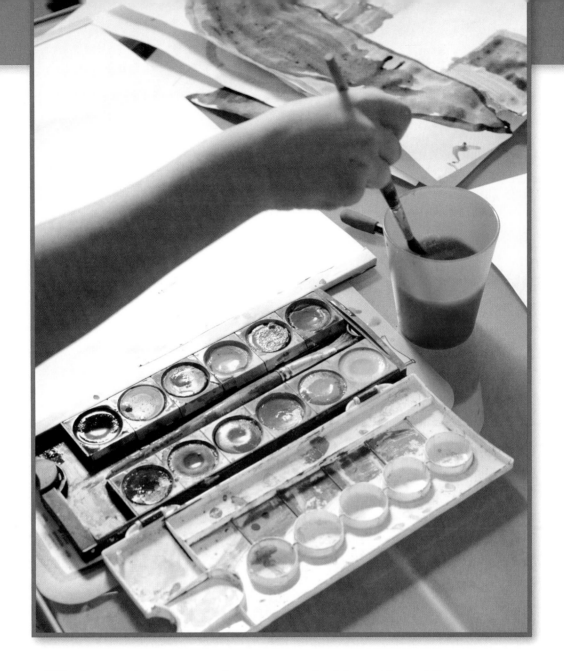

Thinking about Mix It Up!

1. Tell about a mixture of solids.

2. Tell about a mixture of liquids.

3. Tell about a mixture of solids and liquids.

Have you ever had a glass of lemonade on a hot summer day? After you drink the lemonade, ice is left in the glass. After a while, the ice turns to water. Do you know what happened? The ice **melted**.

When a solid melts, it changes from a solid to a liquid.

Other solids can melt, too. Butter is a solid. But if you **heat** the butter, it melts. Solids melt when they get hot.

Liquids can change to solids, too. Do you know how?

Think about making ice cubes. You pour water in a tray. Then, you put it in a cold place. When the water gets very cold, you have solid ice cubes! When a liquid **cools** or **freezes**, it changes to a solid.

Can you think of other liquids that turn to solid?

Liquid chocolate turns to solid as it cools. Liquid chocolate can be poured into molds. When the chocolate cools, it is solid. That's how candy is made into different shapes!

This candle is melting and freezing at the same time. The wax near the flame gets hot. It melts and turns to liquid. Some of the liquid wax burns to make the flame. Some of the liquid wax flows down the side of the candle. When the liquid wax is away from the heat, it cools and freezes back into solid wax.

Thinking about Heating and Cooling

1. Tell about how solids change into liquids.

2. Tell about how liquids change into solids.

3. The ice in the picture above is melting. Why?

Is Change Reversible?

Place an ice cube in a bowl on a table. The solid ice will melt. It will change into liquid water. Put the water in a very cold freezer. The liquid water will freeze. It will change back into solid ice.

This change between solid and liquid is **reversible**. *Reverse* means to go the other way. Heating can change water from a solid to a liquid. Cooling can change it back to a solid.

What other materials freeze and melt like water? What other changes are reversible?

How do you make pancakes? Mix flour, milk, egg, and a little oil to make batter. Batter is a thick liquid.

Pour some batter on a hot griddle. After a few minutes, the pancake is ready to eat. The hot pancake is a solid object. The liquid batter changed into a solid. Is making pancakes reversible? No, the pancake cannot change back to batter.

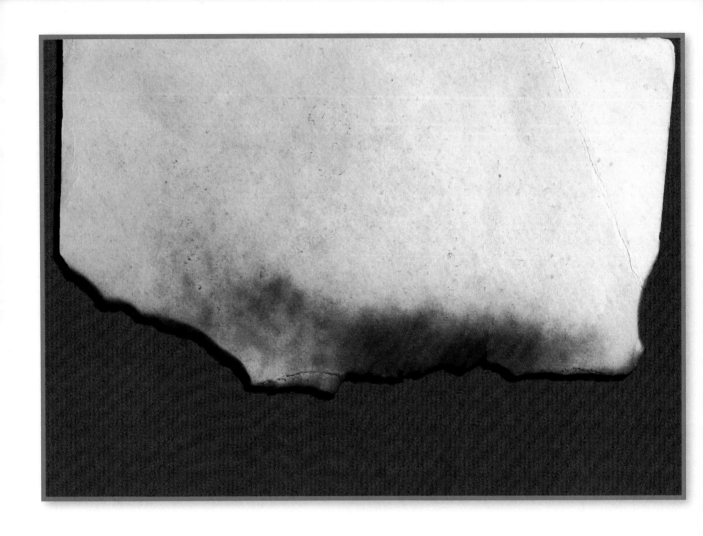

Paper is a solid material. What happens to
paper when you heat it? Does it melt like
ice and turn into liquid? When you put
paper on a hot surface, it changes color.
Paper might turn brown.

With more heat, the paper starts to burn. A little bit of ash remains after the paper burns up. Burning paper is a change that is not reversible.

Did you ever drop a fresh egg? A fresh egg is liquid inside.

Boil an egg in water for a few minutes, and the egg cooks.

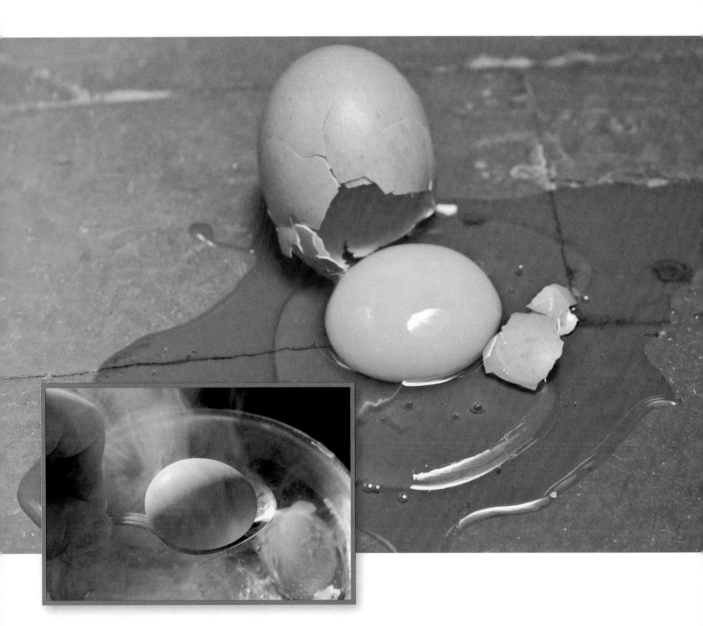

When you crack the shell, the egg inside is solid. A cooked egg changes from liquid to solid.

Does cooling the cooked egg change it back into liquid? No, cooking an egg is a change that is not reversible.

Thinking about Is Change Reversible?

1. What happens when ice cream warms? Is its state reversible?

2. Chocolate can be a liquid or a solid. How can you reverse its state?

3. Explain how the change in a wax candle is reversible. Explain when the change is not reversible.

4. Describe another example of a change caused by heat that is not reversible.

FOSS Science Resources

Pebbles, Sand, and Silt

Table of Contents

Exploring Rocks

Think about a **rock**. A rock has
many **properties**. What does
the rock look like?

Rocks can be small or large. They can be heavy or light. They can be smooth or rough. They can be round or flat, shiny or dull. Rocks can be different in many ways.

Some rocks are too big to hold in
your hand. A rock can be as big
as a mountain!

Other rocks are so small that you can hold thousands in your hand. Look at the picture of a **sand dune**. Can you see the tiny rocks blowing in the **wind**?

Rocks of all sizes can be found in rivers.
Over time, rocks in a river become
smooth. Rocks become smooth from
rubbing against one another.

Rocks of all sizes can be found in a desert, too.
How big is the rock you're thinking of?

Rocks can be many different colors. They can be black, brown, red, or white. They might even be pink or green. Some rocks have speckles or stripes, too.

Rocks can be many different sizes. They can have different **textures**. They can be many colors and shapes. They can even have patterns.

What does the rock you're thinking about look like?

Colorful Rocks

What are these colorful objects?

They are **minerals**. There are many different kinds of minerals. Minerals come in lots of different colors.

Rocks are made out of minerals.
That's why rocks can be so many
different colors.

This rock is made of different minerals. Can you see them?

Look for the black mineral. Look for the pink mineral. Look for the gray mineral. These are the minerals in this rock. This rock is called pink **granite**.

The Story of Sand

Have you ever looked at one grain of **sand** and thought, "I wonder how it got so small?"

A grain of sand wasn't always so small! It might have once been part of a **boulder**. The boulder could have broken off a mountain. The boulder could have tumbled down the mountain.

Maybe the boulder rolled into a river.
Water in a river can move rocks. The rocks
bump together in the water. The boulder
might have broken into **cobbles** and
pebbles. Cobbles are bigger than pebbles.

Maybe the river carried the pebbles to the ocean. Ocean waves crash over pebbles. The pebbles might have broken into **gravel**. Pebbles are bigger than gravel.

Wind and water move and rub rocks together. Over time, rocks break apart. They can get smaller and smaller. They can break into very tiny rocks. This is called **weathering**. These tiny rocks are grains of sand.

Compare the sand from different places.

Corpus Christi, Texas

Dawson City, Texas

Green Sands Bay, Hawaii

Plum Island, Massachusetts

Cape Hatteras National Seashore, North Carolina

Dix Beach, North Carolina

Next time you build a sand castle, think about
the story of sand!

Thinking about The Story of Sand

1. Put these rocks in order by size, from the largest to the smallest.

        sand

        boulder

        gravel

        cobble

        pebble

2. Tell the story of sand.

Rocks Move

Water and wind move rocks of all sizes.

Look at the pictures on these two pages. Can you tell what moved the rocks?

Mudflat

Sandy Beach

Washout

Landforms

Some landforms are formed by eruption.

A **volcano** is a place where lava, ash, and **gases** escape from openings in Earth's crust.

A cinder cone is a kind of volcano. It forms when cinders (pieces of lava) burst out of Earth in an eruption.

A shield volcano forms from flowing lava that has cooled. It is wider than it is tall.

A composite volcano forms from different kinds of eruptions. Layers of cinders, lava, and ash build up into a mountain.

Some landforms are formed by weathering and erosion.

A **valley** is a low area between mountains. Rivers make V-shaped valleys. Glaciers make U-shaped valleys.

A **canyon** is a deep V-shaped valley. Rivers erode the steep sides of canyons.

A **mesa** is a wide, flat-topped hill. It has at least one steep side.

A **butte** is a hill with steep sides and a flat top.
A butte is smaller than a mesa.

A **beach** is an area at the edge of a lake or the ocean. Beaches are often sandy.

A **delta** is a fan-shaped deposit of earth materials. Deltas form at the mouth of a river or stream.

A **plain** is low, flat, level land. Plains are found in the center of the United States.

A sand dune is a mound or hill of sand formed by wind.

Some landforms rise above Earth's surface. They weather to create other landforms.

A **mountain** is a high, steep area of land. Some mountains are volcanoes, but not this one.

A **plateau** is an area of high, nearly flat land. Plateaus cover a lot of area.

Making Things with Rocks

People use rocks to make things. A quarry is a place where people dig rocks out of the ground.

Big pieces of rock are used to make big things.
Statues and churches are often made from rock.
People make things out of rock because it lasts
a long time.

Pebbles and gravel are part of the mixture
called **asphalt**. Asphalt is used to pave
streets and playgrounds.

Gravel and sand are used to make sidewalks. The gravel and sand are mixed together with **cement** and water. Cement is like glue. It holds the mixture together. When the mixture gets hard, it makes **concrete**.

Even the tiniest rocks are useful. **Clay** is made up of rocks that are tinier than sand! They are so small that you can't see only one rock with your eyes. People mold clay into many shapes.

Clay is used to make bricks. Bricks are used to
make walls and buildings. Bricks are used to
make walking paths, too.

The bricks are held together with concrete
mortar. Look at the mortar between the bricks.
It is made of cement and sand.

Some bricks are made of concrete. They are called cinder blocks. How are cinder blocks and bricks the same? How are they different?

Whatever their size, rocks are useful. People make lasting and beautiful things from rocks.

What Are Natural Resources?

Rocks are **natural resources**. Rock walls can be formed by nature. Rock walls can be made by people, too.

Look at the rock walls. Which ones are natural? Which ones are made by people?

Stepping stones and walking paths can be natural. Stepping stones and walking paths can be made by people, too.

Look at the walking paths. Which ones are natural? Which ones are made by people?

121

Rock gardens can be natural. Rock gardens can be made by people, too.

Look at the rock gardens. Which ones are natural? Which ones are made by people?

123

What Is in Soil?

Rocks are all around you. The **soil** under your feet has rocks in it. Some of the tiny rocks and minerals in soil are called **silt**. Silt is smaller than sand, but bigger than clay. Sand, clay, gravel, and pebbles can be in soil, too.

When plants and animals die, they become part of the soil. Plants and animals **decay** into tiny pieces called **humus**. Humus provides **nutrients** for plants. It also helps the soil **retain** water.

What is this animal that lives in soil? A worm! Worms are good for soil. They burrow through the soil. They break it apart and enrich the humus. Worms help plants grow by mixing and turning the soil.

Not all soil is alike. Some soil has more humus. Some has more clay or sand. Some has more pebbles and gravel. What differences do you see in these soils?

Testing Soil

Do plants grow better in soil or sand? Here's what you can do to find out.

1. Get four cups that are all the same size.

2. Fill two cups with potting soil that has lots of humus. Fill the other two cups with sand.

3. Plant three sunflower seeds in each cup.

4. Put the same amount of water in each cup.

5. Keep the cups in a sunny window, and record what happens.

Thinking about Testing Soil

1. Is this a good way to test the question?

2. Two students planted seeds in soil and sand. Look at the plants above. Which seeds grew better? Why do you think that happened?

3. Do the test yourself. Draw or write about your results.

Where Is Water Found?

Water is found everywhere on Earth.
Water is part of every living thing. Every
plant and animal is made of water. Even
you are mostly made of water!

Fresh water is found in streams and rivers. Streams can be small like a creek. Rivers are larger streams of water.

Streams and rivers bring water into and out of ponds and lakes.

Fresh water is found in ponds and lakes, too. Ponds are small bodies of water. Lakes are larger and deeper bodies of water.

The water moves slowly in ponds and lakes. Sand and silt settle to the bottom of ponds and lakes.

Fresh water is our most important natural resource. Plants and animals need water to live and grow.

People use water to drink, cook, and wash.
People use water to grow food and to power
factories, too.

Most of the water on Earth is **salt water**.
Salt water is found in seas and the ocean.
The ocean is the largest body of salt water.
Seas are smaller than the ocean.

Salt water is found in salt marshes. They are
muddy places next to seas. Salt marshes have
lots of grasses and small plants. Salt marshes
have slow-moving water.

Salt water is found in mangrove forests. They are like salt marshes, but they have trees and bushes. The roots of mangrove trees help protect the shore.

Salt water is found in coral reefs. Coral reefs grow in warm, shallow seas. Coral reefs are made from corals. Corals are the hard parts of sea animals.

Salt water is found on sandy beaches and rocky shores, too. You can see the ocean water move back and forth in waves on beaches and shores.

Where is fresh water found in your community?

Where is salt water found in your community?

States of Water

Liquid water is one state of water. We can pour it into a glass to drink. We spray it from a hose to water plants. Liquid water can drip from a fountain.

We see liquid water as dewdrops in the morning.
We see it as rain falling to Earth, too.

Solid ice is another state of water. When it gets cold, water freezes into a solid. We can pack snow to make a snowball. We can catch a snowflake.

We can skate on ice. We can float
ice cubes in lemonade.

Gas is another state of water. We cannot
see water when it is a gas. But it is in the
air all around us. When the gas becomes
a liquid, we see it as a cloud or rain.

When the liquid becomes a solid, we see water as snow or hail.

Water is found in all three states on Earth.
Water can be a solid, a liquid, and a gas.

Can you see all three states of water here?

Erosion

What happened to this road? People once drove on this road. During a big storm, waves crashed against the shore. They washed away the soil under the road. Parts of the road were destroyed.

Waves are moving water that cause **erosion**
on a coast. Ocean waves often erode the shore
during storms. Coastal erosion can damage
roads and buildings. Waves can also wash
away all the sand on a beach.

Where else do we find moving water? Water flows downhill in rivers and streams. Heavy rain causes the water in streams and rivers to flood their banks. Fast flowing water erodes the banks.

Engineers designed a strong barrier for the bank
of this river. The barrier will protect the road and
buildings from erosion caused by flowing water.

It will block rainwater from the road. It will stop
the river from flooding the road.

Look for different ways that people protect the edges of waterways from erosion. Some design solutions use heavy objects to cover soil and hold it in place.

Sandbags

Concrete shapes

Concrete bricks

Cattails

Bundles of sticks

Bundles of sticks can protect riverbanks from
moving water. Another good way to protect
banks against erosion is to grow water
plants, like cattails, along the banks.

Moving water is not the only force that causes erosion. Moving air can cause erosion, too. Powerful winds can remove topsoil from a farm. The winds lift the valuable topsoil into the air and carry it far away.

Beaches can be eroded by wind, too. Strong
winds that blow across a beach can lift sand
onto nearby land.

People have learned how to slow down erosion of topsoil and beach sand. Farmers plant rows of trees or shrubs to block the wind near their fields.

People put low wooden fences on the beach to slow the blowing sand. The wind piles the sand up by the fences and makes dunes. Once dunes form high on the beach, beach grass can grow. The grass on the dunes slows erosion even more.

These two roads have problems. What problems can you see? What might have caused the erosion? What would you suggest as a solution for the problem?

Ways to Represent Land and Water

How would you describe your classroom to your grandparents? You could tell them it has eight tables, each with four chairs. You could tell them what the furniture looks like. You could show them a photograph, but a photograph might not show everything.

You could draw a picture to represent the classroom. The drawing might show the size, design, and location of some of the furniture.

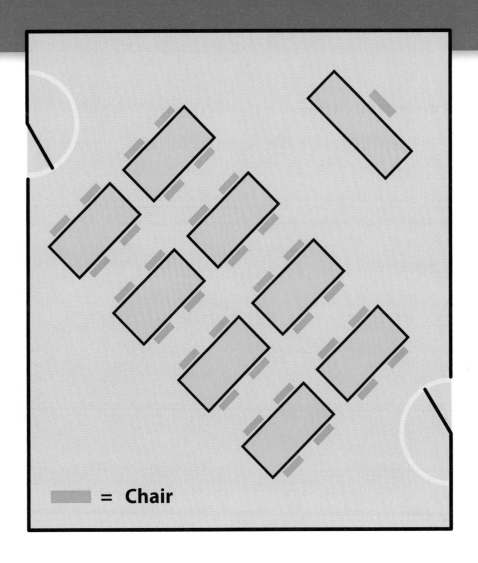

= **Chair**

You could also provide a **map** of the classroom. A map could show where all the tables and chairs are in the room. A map is a view from directly overhead.

These ways to represent a room are also good ways to represent Earth's surface. You can use photographs, drawings, and maps to show the location, size, and kinds of land and water in an area.

This photograph shows Crater Lake in Oregon.
It is the deepest lake in the United States,
594 meters deep.

A drawing is a different way to show Crater Lake.

A map is a different way to represent
Crater Lake. The map shows the shape of
the lake. It shows roads and other nearby
features surrounding the lake.

Crater Lake

Wizard Island

This photograph shows Mount Shasta. Mount Shasta is a volcano in Northern California. It is very tall, 4,322 meters.

A drawing is another way to show Mount Shasta.

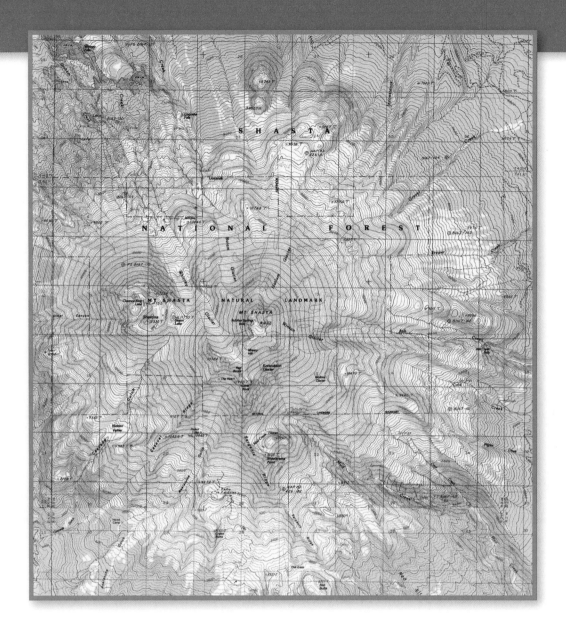

This map shows a topographic view of Mount Shasta. The lines show how high the land is. You can think of them as steps. The steps go up to the very top of the mountain. Water, streams, and ice appear in blue. Areas with trees are green. Maps can show a lot of information.

This photograph shows the Scioto River flowing through the city of Columbus, Ohio. This part of the river bank has a park. The park is called Scioto Mile.

This drawing is a different way to show the park.

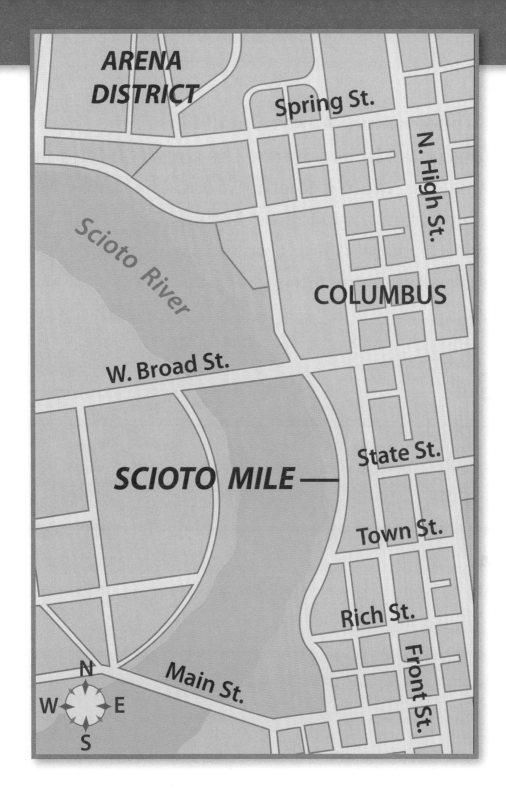

A map of the park shows how big the park is and where it is in Columbus.

This photograph shows a small part of the Great Plains in the United States. The circles and squares are fields of grain and other crops. The crops are watered from the Ogallala Aquifer. The Ogallala Aquifer is huge. It holds water in the ground underneath eight states.

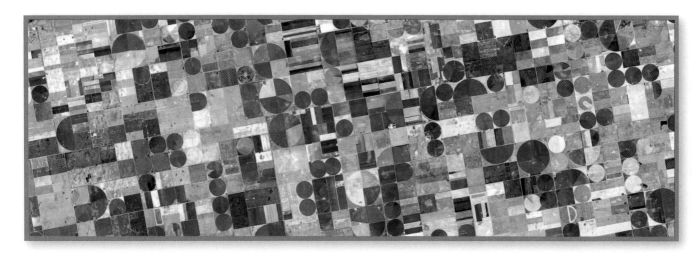

This drawing shows the pattern of crops above the Ogallala Aquifer.

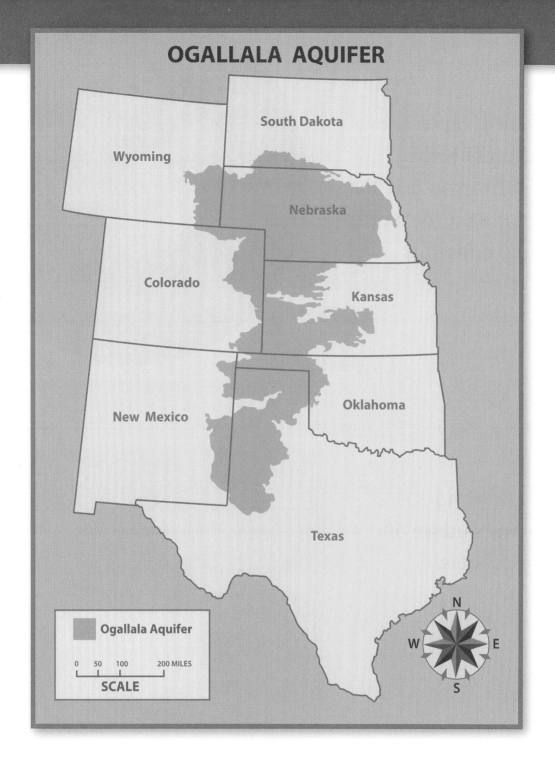

OGALLALA AQUIFER

South Dakota

Wyoming

Nebraska

Colorado

Kansas

New Mexico

Oklahoma

Texas

Ogallala Aquifer

0 50 100 200 MILES

SCALE

N
W   E
S

This map shows how big the aquifer is. It is located under parts of Oklahoma, Texas, New Mexico, Colorado, Kansas, Nebraska, Wyoming, and South Dakota.

This image of Earth shows the location of North America. Can you find the United States on the North American continent?

Here is a drawing showing the outline of the United States.

This map shows part of the United States, outlining 48 states. It also shows highways that connect the states, and large waterways (lakes, rivers, and the ocean).

Life Science

FOSS Science Resources

Insects and Plants

Table of Contents

Animals and Plants in Their Habitats

Look at this **grassland habitat**. Do you see anything **living** here? Let's take a closer look.

Look! A grasshopper sits in the green grass. Grass **plants** and grasshoppers are living in this grassland habitat. Grass and grasshoppers get their **basic needs** met in the grassland habitat.

Land **animals** need food, water, air, space, shelter, and a comfortable temperature. Grasshoppers eat grass for food and water. In the grass, grasshoppers have air and shelter. In summer, the grassland provides a warm habitat for **insects**, like grasshoppers, and other animals, like prairie dogs.

Plants need water, air, sunlight, and **nutrients**. Grass gets water and nutrients from the rich, moist grassland soil. Their roots take up water and nutrients. Air flows around the grass. Grass uses sunlight to make the food it needs to live.

Other parts of the country are different from the grassland habitat. This is a **desert** habitat. What do you see living here? Let's take a closer look.

Plants and animals are living in the desert, too.
How do they get the things they need to live?

Desert plants get water and nutrients from the
desert soil. The plants have large root systems to
collect water. Some desert plants, like cactuses,
have thick spongy stems. Cactus stems store
water for the plant to use later.

The Sun shines brightly on the desert most of the time. Air flows easily around the desert plants. Deserts are very hot during the summer. But desert plants can live even in very hot temperatures.

Some desert animals eat other animals for food. Some desert animals eat **seeds** for food. Harvester ants gather seeds. They store the seeds to eat during the year. Ants get water from the seeds they eat.

Ants dig tunnels and chambers. Their underground tunnels give ants a safe space to live. The tunnels provide shelter for the ants so they can **survive** the hot desert summer.

This is a **tundra** habitat in winter.
Some parts of Alaska have this kind
of habitat. What do you see living
here? Let's take a closer look.

Tundra plants survive the winter in a resting stage. When the Sun warms the land, the plants begin to grow again. The plants take up water and nutrients from melting ice and snow. They use sunlight to make their food. Tundra plants can survive cold temperatures.

Caribou roam the open space of the tundra. They eat the short plants. They drink from pools of melted snow. Caribou have thick fur to protect them from the cold temperature. But the fur is not thick enough to protect them from mosquitoes.

Mosquitoes burrow down in tundra plants in the fall. They rest there during the cold winter. When the snow melts in spring, the mosquitoes look for food and mates. The female mosquitoes lay **eggs** on pools of water.

After the eggs hatch, mosquito **larvae** eat tiny bits of food in the water. The mosquito larvae grow quickly for a few weeks. Then they swim to the surface of the water and break out of their old skin. Now they are **adult** mosquitoes and fly to find food.

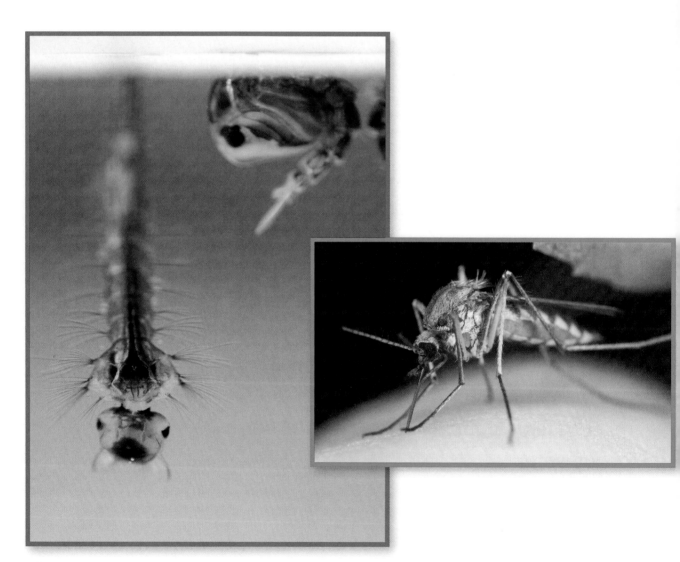

When you look closely at a habitat, you will
find animals and plants living there. Living
things **thrive** when they have what they
need to live.

Flowers and Seeds

These are wild brassica plants. Each plant grows a lot of **flowers**. But brassica plants do not grow flowers to look pretty. The flowers are an important part of the plant's **life cycle**.

Soon, the flowers fade and dry up.
Something new appears right where
each flower once grew. It looks like a
little green bean. It is a seedpod.

Weeks later, the seedpods are big and dry.
There are about six seeds inside each seedpod.
What do you think will happen if someone
plants the new seeds?

Brassica plants are not the only plants that make seeds. Cherry trees make seeds. Where are they found?

There is one seed inside each cherry. And where does the cherry grow? It grows right where the cherry flower was.

Plants grow flowers. The flowers grow into **fruit**. Fruit have seeds inside. When the seeds grow into new plants, it is called **reproduction**.

Apple tree

Apple flowers

Apple seeds

Apple fruit

Have you ever seen tomato
flowers? Tomato flowers grow
into tomatoes. Tomatoes are
fruit. They have seeds.

Can you see the strawberry flowers?
Strawberry flowers grow into fruit.
Strawberries have seeds, too.

New plants grow from seeds. Seeds are found in fruit. Fruit grow out of flowers. Flowers and fruit are important in the life cycles of plants.

Thinking about Flowers and Seeds

1. Name one plant, and tell about its flowers.

2. Where are the seeds on a brassica plant?

3. Name two fruits you like to eat.

4. Name the parts of a plant that are important for its life cycle.

How Seeds Travel

How can we make sure plants have
the space they need? Get rid of weeds!
Weeds are unwanted plants.

How do weeds get into gardens?

Most weeds start as seeds. Seeds come
from flowers. First, the seeds get ripe.
Then, they are ready to travel!

Some seeds glide or spin in air. They might land far away. If they land on moist soil, they can grow.

Some seeds are carried by animals. These seeds have little hooks. The hooks can hold onto an animal's fur. The seeds go where the animal goes.

Some seeds can even be carried by you!
They can stick to your sweater or shoes.
Some seeds will fall off. When they land
on moist soil, they can sprout and grow.

Birds and squirrels can move seeds, too. Birds eat berries and fly away. There are seeds inside the berries. The seeds pass through the birds. Now the seeds are in new places!

Squirrels eat seeds, too. They hide acorns to eat during winter. Lost and forgotten acorns can grow into oak trees. Seeds travel in many ways.

Now can you tell how weeds get into gardens?

Thinking about
How Seeds Travel

1. How do seeds travel in air?

2. How do seeds with hooks travel?

3. How do birds move seeds?

4. How do squirrels move seeds?

So Many Kinds, So Many Places

This amazing animal is an insect. Flies, ants, and crickets are all insects, too. There are so many kinds of insects. Insects are everywhere! Can you name some others?

No matter where you are, an insect is probably near you. Insects are in the air and in the water. Some creep in the Arctic snow. Others scamper around in the desert.

These ladybugs have gathered on a tree trunk. Some insects live on the tops of mountains. Other insects live in the rain forest. Insects are everywhere!

Insects might seem like pests to you. Some insects eat clothes, buildings, and crops. But insects are very important. Many different animals need them for food.

Insects are important for people, too. Bees move **pollen** from one flower to another, and that allows plants to grow fruit and seeds. Bees also make sweet honey.

People use thread from the cocoon of the silkworm to make clothing.

Next time you go outside, look for insects. They are everywhere!

Thinking about So Many Kinds, So Many Places

1. What are some ways insects are important to humans?

2. What are some ways insects are important to other animals?

Insect Shapes and Colors

Insects are different shapes and colors. The shape or color can help insects hide. An enemy might not see an insect that looks like its habitat. A hungry bird or lizard might think this insect is a leaf.

This praying mantis hides in the leaves, waiting to catch an insect to eat.

The walking sticks on this twig are very hard to see. Can you find them?

Look at the bright colors and design on this butterfly. Do you think it is hiding from its enemies?

Some insects are very easy to see. They are very colorful. They might have special markings.

Brightly colored insects often taste bad. They make other animals sick. Animals learn to stay away!

The spots on this beetle look like huge eyes.
A hungry animal might think the beetle is
a much bigger insect. The animal might be
scared away.

Insect Life Cycles

Insects might look different at each stage of their lives. Most insects go through four stages. The stages are egg, larva, **pupa**, and adult. The eggs of this insect were laid inside cells.

After a few days, a larva hatches from each egg. The tiny larva stays curled up inside the cell. The larva eats food made from pollen and honey. This food makes the larva grow.

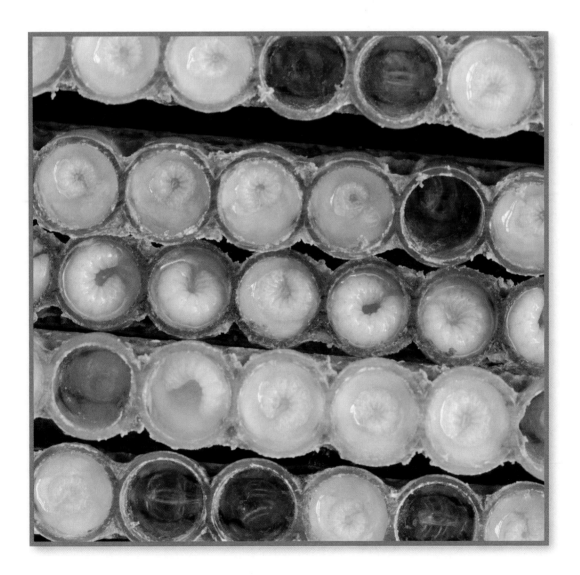

Then, the cell is covered with wax. Inside the cell, each larva turns into a pupa.

In the pupa stage, the insect goes through a big change. Soon, an adult crawls out of each cell. Do you know what insect this is?

It's a bee! After a short rest, the bee can go right to work. Young adult bees work in the hive. Older bees work outside the hive.

The larvae of different insects do not look the same.
These larvae will become insects you know well.
What will they look like as adults?

Moths and mosquitoes!

Some kinds of insects don't have larvae or pupae. When they hatch from eggs, they are called **nymphs**. Many nymphs look like their parents, but smaller.

Milkweed bugs go through four nymph stages.
In each new stage, they look more like an adult.
How many different nymph stages can you find?

Thinking about Insect Life Cycles

1. Tell about the life cycle of a bee.

2. Tell about the life cycle of a milkweed bug.

Life Goes Around

On a lucky day, you might see a ladybug.
A ladybug is red with black spots. This is
an adult ladybug. But have you ever seen
a baby ladybug?

Adult ladybugs mate. Then, the female lays eggs. When an egg hatches, a larva comes out. The black larva is a baby ladybug. But it doesn't look like its parents. The larva eats and grows for about 4 weeks.

Then, the larva **pupates**. Inside the pupa, the larva is changing. When the pupa opens, an adult ladybug comes out. It is red with black spots. Now it looks just like its parents.

The ladybug life cycle is like the life cycle of many other insects. It is like the life cycle of mealworms. It is like the life cycle of butterflies and moths. But it is different from the life cycle of some other animals.

Some animals hatch from eggs. Some animals are born alive. They all grow up to be adults. The adults mate and have babies called **offspring**.

Every animal goes around the life cycle. Cycle means to go around. The life cycle of a robin looks like this.

Robin eggs

Baby robins

Young robin

Adult robin

Trout lay eggs in streams. After 6 to 8 weeks, the eggs hatch. Tiny, fat babies swim out. You can see that they are fish. But they don't look like their parents yet.

For the next year, they grow up little by little. In 2 years, they are adults. They look just like their parents. They mate and lay eggs in streams. Can you describe the trout life cycle?

Frogs lay eggs in water, too. When an egg
hatches, a tadpole swims out. It looks more
like a fish with a big head than a frog. It
doesn't look like its parents yet.

The tadpole eats and grows. In a few weeks, the tadpole starts to change. Its long, flat tail gets shorter. Its legs start to grow.

In a few more weeks, the tadpole has grown into a frog. It looks just like its parents. Can you describe the frog life cycle?

Ducks lay eggs in a nest in a **marsh**. The mother duck sits on the eggs to keep them warm. When they hatch, the babies are fluffy and yellow. The babies are called ducklings. You can see that they are ducks. But they don't look like their parents yet.

The ducklings eat and grow. In a few weeks, they get their brown feathers. In a few months, they are adults. They look just like their parents. In the next year, the adult ducks will mate. They will raise new families of ducklings. Can you describe the duck life cycle?

Mice do not lay eggs. Baby mice grow inside
the mother. The babies are born alive. Newborn
mice are pink, hairless, and blind. You can see
that they are mice. But they don't look like their
parents yet.

In a few days, the babies open their eyes. Their fur starts to grow. In a few months, they will be adults. They will be ready to continue the life cycle. They will have babies of their own. Can you describe the life cycle of mice?

Thinking about Life Goes Around

1. Does a ladybug larva look like its parents?

2. Tell about the life cycle of a ladybug.

3. Tell about the life cycle of a different animal.

4. Name five animals that hatch from eggs.

5. Name three animals that are born alive (not from eggs).

References

References

Science Safety Rules

1. Listen carefully to your teacher's instructions. Follow all directions. Ask questions if you don't know what to do.

2. Tell your teacher if you have any allergies.

3. Never put any materials in your mouth. Do not taste anything unless your teacher tells you to do so.

4. Never smell any unknown material. If your teacher tells you to smell something, wave your hand over the material to bring the smell toward your nose.

5. Do not touch your face, mouth, ears, eyes, or nose while working with chemicals, plants, or animals.

6. Always protect your eyes. Wear safety goggles when necessary. Tell your teacher if you wear contact lenses.

7. Always wash your hands with soap and warm water after handling chemicals, plants, or animals.

8. Never mix any chemicals unless your teacher tells you to do so.

9. Report all spills, accidents, and injuries to your teacher.

10. Treat animals with respect, caution, and consideration.

11. Clean up your work space after each investigation.

12. Act responsibly during all science activities.

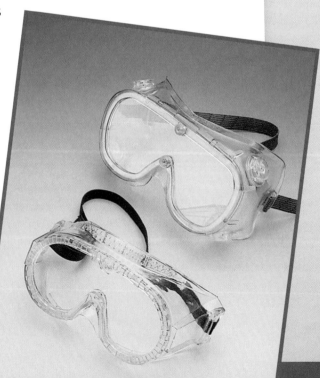

Glossary

adult a fully grown organism **(190)**

air a mixture of gases that we breathe. Air is one of the four most important needs for any organism. **(8)**

animal a living thing that is not a plant **(179)**

asphalt a mixture of pebbles and gravel **(113)**

basic need something that is needed for plants and animals to survive. Plants and animals need air, water, food, space, shelter, and light. **(178)**

beach an area at the edge of a lake or the ocean **(108)**

boulder a very large rock that is bigger than a cobble **(95)**

bridge a structure that connects landmasses over water **(28)**

bubbly describes a liquid that is full of bubbles **(52)**

butte a hill with steep sides and flat top **(107)**

canyon a deep V-shaped valley **(106)**

cement a finely ground powder that is like glue when mixed with water **(114)**

clay rocks that are smaller than sand and silt. It is hard to see just one. **(115)**

cobble a rock that is smaller than a boulder, but bigger than a pebble **(96)**

concrete a mixture of gravel, sand, cement, and water **(114)**

cool to make something colder **(66)**

crystal the shape of salt after evaporation **(60)**

decay when dead plants or animals break down into small pieces **(125)**

delta earth materials built up in the shape of a fan **(108)**

desert a dry place with little rain **(181)**

dissolve when a solid is mixed with a liquid, and the solid breaks apart into pieces so tiny they can't be seen in the liquid **(59)**

egg the first stage of a life cycle **(189)**

erosion the carrying away of earth materials by water, wind, or ice **(149)**

evaporate when a liquid dries up, goes into the air as a gas, and can't be seen **(60)**

fabric a flexible material used to make clothing. Fabric and cloth are the same. **(16)**

flower the part of a plant that grows into fruit **(192)**

foamy describes a liquid that has a layer of bubbles on top **(52)**

freeze to change a liquid to a solid by cooling it **(66)**

fresh water water without salt. Fresh water is found in streams, lakes, and rivers. **(131)**

fruit the part of a plant with seeds in it. Flowers grow into fruit, and fruit produce seeds in plant reproduction. **(196)**

gas matter that can't be seen but is all around. Air is an example of a gas. **(6, 104)**

granite the name of a kind of rock. Pink granite is made of four minerals. Those minerals are hornblende (black), mica (black), feldspar (pink), and quartz (gray). **(93)**

grassland a place with a lot of grass and often no trees **(177)**

gravel a rock that is smaller than a pebble, but bigger than sand **(97)**

habitat the place or natural area where plants or animals live **(177)**

heat to make something warmer **(65)**

humus bits of dead plant and animal parts in the soil **(125)**

insect an animal that has six legs and three main body parts. They are the head, thorax, and abdomen. **(179)**

larva (plural **larvae**) a stage in the insect life cycle after hatching from eggs. Insect larvae look different from their parents and are often wormlike. **(190)**

life cycle the stages in the life of a plant or animal **(192)**

liquid matter that flows freely and takes the shape of its container **(6, 141)**

living alive **(177)**

map a picture that shows different parts of something **(161)**

marsh soft, wet land that is sometimes covered with water **(238)**

material what something is made of **(15)**

matter anything that takes up space **(5)**

melt to change a solid to a liquid by heating it **(64)**

mesa a hill with a wide, flat top **(107)**

mineral the colorful ingredient that makes up rocks **(91)**

mixture two or more materials put together **(56)**

mortar a mixture of cement and sand **(116)**

mountain a high and steep area of land **(110)**

natural resource something from Earth. Rocks, soil, air, and water are natural resources. **(118)**

nutrient something that living things need to grow and stay healthy **(125, 180)**

nymph a stage in the insect life cycle that has no larva or pupa. Nymphs look like their parents, but are smaller. **(226)**

object a solid thing **(14)**

offspring a new plant or animal produced by a parent **(233)**

particle a tiny piece of a material **(41)**

pebble a rock that is smaller than a cobble, but bigger than gravel **(96)**

plain a low, flat, level area of land **(109)**

plant a living thing that has roots, stems, and leaves. Plants make their own food. **(178)**

plateau a high, nearly flat area of land **(110)**

pollen a fine powder produced by flowers. Pollen is needed to produce fruit and seeds. **(213)**

property something that you can observe about an object or a material. Size, color, shape, texture, and smell are properties. **(16, 83)**

pupa (plural **pupae**) a stage in the insect life cycle between the larva and adult stages **(220)**

pupate to change into a pupa **(231)**

reproduction the process of producing offspring **(196)**

retain to hold **(125)**

reversible to change back to the original state **(71)**

rock a solid earth material. Rocks are made of minerals. **(83)**

salt water water with salt. Salt water is found in seas and the ocean. **(135)**

sand rocks that are smaller than gravel, but bigger than silt **(94)**

sand dune a hill of sand formed by wind **(86)**

seed the part of a plant found inside fruit. Seeds can grow into new plants. **(184)**

silt rocks that are smaller than sand, but bigger than clay **(124)**

sink to fall or drop to the bottom **(43)**

soil a mix of sand, silt, clay, gravel, pebbles, and humus **(124)**

solid matter that holds its own shape and always takes up the same amount of spac **(6, 143)**

state one of the three groups of matter: solid, liquid, or gas **(6)**

surface the top layer of something **(37)**

survive to stay alive **(185)**

texture the way something feels **(90)**

thrive to grow fast and stay healthy **(191)**

tower a tall structure **(24)**

translucent describes a liquid or solid that is clear enough to let light through but is not clear enough to see something on the other side **(52)**

transparent describes a liquid or solid that you can see through easily **(21)**

tundra a place in the arctic or high on mountains **(186)**

valley a low area between mountains **(106)**

viscous describes a liquid that is thick and slow moving **(52)**

volcano a place where lava, ash, and gases come out from the earth **(104)**

weathering when rocks break apart over time to become smaller and smaller **(98)**

wind moving air **(86)**

Photo Credits